SO-AAZ-082

TRADITIONAL PORTUGUESE RECIPES from PROVINCETOWN

by Mary Alice Cook

edited by
Gillian Drake

published by
SHANK PAINTER PUBLISHING COMPANY
Provincetown, Mass.

**Dedicated to the memory of
my Father, Mother and Sister
(Manuel, Alice and Jocelyn Lewis)**

The editor wishes to thank Grace Goveia Collinson,
Fred Hemley and Adrienne Moy for their help.

Copies of this book may be ordered from
Shank Painter Publishing Company
650 Commercial Street, Provincetown, MA 02657
(508) 487-9169
Please send $7.50 plus $1.50 shipping

The photographs in this book are all historic pictures of old Provincetown, many taken by George Elmer Browne, a painter living in Provincetown in the first half of this century. He operated the West End School of Painting in Provincetown, as well as a painting school in New York City, and was Vice President of the Provincetown Art Association. These photographs were taken by him circa 1915 and were restored and reproduced by Fred Hemley. All other photographs are from the photo album of Mary Alice Cook.

© Mary Alice Cook and Gillian H. Drake, 1983

All rights reserved. This book, or parts thereof, may not be
reproduced in any form without permission of the publisher.

I.S.B.N. # 0-9609814-3-8

Printed by Shank Painter Printing Company, Provincetown, Mass. 02657

INTRODUCTION

To understand and fully appreciate the early Portuguese of Provincetown and their ways, it is important to note that they were divided into three groups—the continentals, locally known as "Lisbons"; the Azoreans, often called "St. Michaels"; and natives from the Cape Verde Islands off the coast of Africa, identified also as "Bravas", a name given to them by whaling captains in honor of their great courage. Though these three groups have much in common—for instance, their language, religion and a great love of the sea—they are of quite different ancestry. The continentals of northern Portugal were descendants of Celts and Germans and often had fair complexions and blue eyes, while in the south their blood was a combination of Arab, Barbary, Spanish and French. The Azoreans were basically a mixture of people from Flanders and France, to which was added the blood of seafaring Europeans who chanced to settle on the islands. The Cape Verdeans were descended from white Portuguese, African slaves from the Sudan and Guinea and settlers from middle Europe and Asia.

The first Portuguese to come in numbers to Provincetown were the Cape Verdeans, brought over by whaling captains in the early part of the 19th century at the heyday of the whaling industry. The captains were finding it increasingly difficult to recruit men from New England for their whaling expeditions, trips that would often last up to two or even three years in length and involved great hardship and danger. So the whale ships would sail with a skeleton crew directly to the Cape Verde Islands to hire young men anxious to see to the world, or, less romantically maybe, to escape conscription. These "Bravas" proved to be ideal workers, earning what was to them great wealth, sufficient to settle in America and take an American wife, or send for a sweeheart from home.

With the discovery of petroleum, the demand for whale products dropped and the whaling industry fell into a decline, forcing the great whaling ships to turn to fishing. The richest fishing grounds on the East Coast were the Grand Banks off the coast of Nova Scotia and fishing boats from all over New England made trips there that often lasted as long as six months. Already fishing the Grand Banks were the Azoreans, followed later by the "Lisbons", both groups being among the earliest Europeans to fish off the coast of Canada. They were impressed by the ways and manners of the American fishermen so that when the chance came, they left their own ships and joined the American "Grand Bankers", many of which hailed from Provincetown, then one of the most important fishing ports in Massachusetts. The Portuguese fishermen settled in Provincetown and they, too, worked hard so they could save enough money to send for their wives and children, as my father did.

As the Portuguese community in Provincetown grew, the families would club together to order foodstuffs from Boston that were essential to their native dishes but not available in the local grocery stores. Even in Boston it was sometimes impossible to obtain the genuine ingredients so foods native to these shores were often substituted in many of the old recipes—for instance, scallops and quahogs are unknown in Portugal, but in Provincetown they feature strongly in the daily fare of the Portuguese. The Portuguese ate basically a vegetarian diet—they grew many of their own vegetables, consumed quantities of fresh and dried fish, and ate very little meat, usually only on special occasions. Many kept pigs from which they made the spicy sausages linguica and chourica. The Portuguese also have a sweet tooth, evidenced by the variety of cookies and pastries they lovingly prepare for feast days, and the famous Portuguese sweet bread. The Cape Verdeans and Azoreans like their food a little spicier than the continentals, and often add vinegar, red pepper, saffron and garlic, singly or collectively, to their dishes.

As the American population of Provincetown acquired a taste for Portuguese food, it began to be served in summer boarding houses and local restaurants. Maline Costa, founder of the Moors Restaurant, was one of the first in town to serve Portuguese food, and his son Mylan traveled to Portugal and the Islands to learn more about Portuguese cuisine; today the Moors serves the most comprehensive selection of this food in town. Although Portuguese food became increasingly popular in Provincetown, no one from the Portuguese community realized that as time went by many of the traditional recipes, most of which were handed down from mother to daughter by word of mouth, would be lost unless they were recorded. Fortunately, Alice Luiz Cook had the foresight to compile a book documenting the authentic Portuguese recipes from her family and friends so that the methods of preparing these dishes are not lost. She is a natural cook like both her parents (in those days a man did not admit to being a good cook), and is now one of the best in Provincetown in my opinion. She is meticulous about the authenticity of the dishes as they were prepared in the old days, even though some may have been adapted to local ingredients.

So it is with great pleasure and pride that I introduce this book written by a compatriot of mine, born in the same little village of Olhao in Portugal, a neighbour of mine in Provincetown for many years, both of us children of immigrants who could barely read or write, both of us graduates of Provincetown High School . . . I applaud her for her wisdom, talent and energy. Our dear neighbors, Tia Anicas, Tia Joaquina,

Emelinda, Tia Adelina, and Estherinha, all excellent cooks and very special people, would have been proud of you too, Alice Luiz Cook.

Graciete Leocadia Gouveia
(Grace Goveia Collinson)

Grace Goveia Collinson was born in Olhao, Portugal in 1908 and came to Provincetown in 1917 during the First World War. Her father was a fisherman who fished on the Grand Banks and he sent for his family to come to America when he had saved enough money to pay for the fares. Grace attended Provincetown High School and then went on to continue her education at the American International College and Mount Holyoke College. She received a Bachelor of Arts degree, one of the first children of Portuguese immigrants in Provincetown to do so (her parents were illiterate). She became a school teacher in Provincetown, a job she held for 26 years, and taught just about every prominent citizen in this town, including two present selectmen and the Superintendent of Provincetown Schools. In 1983 Provincetown voted to honor Grace for her services to the town by naming a town building for her.

A Provincetown Painting

Come with me and see
The most beautiful sunset by the sea
At the very tip of Cape Cod
A painting made only by God.

Its shades of colors and hues
Are a source of joy and good news
Of a day to come, full of sun
Happiness and fun.

Come with me and see
A terrible storm with a raging sea
At the very tip of Cape Cod
A terrifying painting made only by God.

Its dark seas and angry waves
Grip my soul with fear
As I span the stormy waters
At the very tip of Cape Cod.

Have heart, for tommorow, I know
Its blue, beautiful still waters
Will be a joy to behold
At the very tip end of Cape Cod.

Mary Alice Cook, 1977

CONTENTS

SOUPS & APPETIZERS ....Page 15
Kale Soup or Turnip Top Soup, Fish Chowder, Red Bean Soup, Red Beans with Chestnuts and Rice, Cabbage with Red Beans, Chick Pea Soup, Pea Soup, Vegetable Soup, String Bean Soup, Tomato Soup with Toast, Chicken Soup, Horse Beans (Favas).

FISH ....Page 27
Baked Fish, Baked Stuffed Fish, Baked Filet of Flounder, Boiled Fish with Rice, Broiled Fish, Codfish with Chick Peas, Marinated Catfish, Fish Cakes, Monkey Fish Stew (Links), Fish Cheeks and Tongues, Baked Stuffed Quahogs, Rice with Quahogs, Steamed Clams, Clam Fritters, Oyster Stew, Scallop Stew, Scallop Casserole, Rice with Shrimp, Baked Stuffed Shrimp, Boiled Lobster, Lobster Salad, Lobster Stew.

MEAT ....Page 49
Shoulder or Loin of Pork, Marinated, Linguica Cooked Over Hot Coals, Linguica Omelette, Linguica Quiche, Portuguese Chicken Casserole, Smothered Chicken, Frankfurter Stew, Meat Stew, Meat Loaf, Beef Liver.

BREADS ....Page 59
Portuguese Bread, Sweet Bread, Flippers (Fried Dough).

DESSERTS ....Page 65
Portuguese Bread Pudding, Portuguese Sweet Rice Pudding, Portuguese Caramelized Custard ("Flan"), Rolled Cookies (Boles de Folha), Sweet Potato Turnovers (Trutas), Almond Cookies (Bolos d'Amendoas), Egg Cookies (Spreciones), Dreams (Sonhos), Sighs (Suspiros).

CAPE COD FAVORITES...............Page 75

New England Baked Beans, Pot Roast, Apple-Raisin-Cranberry Pie, Blueberry Pie, Beach Plum Jelly, Beach Plum Jelly using Pectin, Beach Plum Jam.

RECIPES FROM MY FRIENDS...........Page 82

Anna's Beach Terrace Chili, Irene's Porcupine Meat Loaf, Jocelyn's Peanut Butter Fudge, Mary's Apricot Squares.

INDEX...................................Page 86

"My father (left) came to America in 1905 . . ."

MY EARLY LIFE

I was born in Olhao, Algarve, Portugal on August 4, 1914 to Manuel and Maria Alice Luiz Perruca.
I came to America, to Provincetown, when I was nine months old. My father came to America in 1905 to go fishing and made several trips back and forth to Portugal. In 1911, he married my mother in Portugal and in 1915 he sent for my mother, my sister Jocelyn and myself. The fishermen who had been here for several years were now making homes for their families and many of these family members came from Portugal on the same ocean liner as we did.

My mother,
Maria Alice Luiz Perruca

My father's last name, Perruca, was dropped when he signed for the draft in 1912. He was told that in America three names were not used, a mistake that was often made with these new "foreigners to America." In truth, the name "Luiz" (Lewis) was his confirmation name, but he became Manuel Luiz and his brother John Gomes Perruca became John Gomes. To this day I am asked why my father's name differs from his blood brother's. Neither my father nor my mother ever returned to their native Portugal. My uncle John, now 96 years old and Provincetown's oldest male resident, also came here in 1905 and has never returned.

I am proud of my Portuguese heritage. I am often asked if I am French, Italian, Greek or Jewish, but seldom if I am Portuguese. In the early 1900s there were many Portuguese families in Provincetown who did not speak English. Their children learned the language at school but still spoke Portuguese at home, otherwise their parents could not understand them. Today, there are very few Portuguese families who still understand or speak their native language. My children who used to speak Portuguese fluently now do not speak it and understand very little. I pride myself that I can still speak the language fluently but I am sorry that my children who spoke Portuguese so well as youngsters cannot speak or understand the language today.

I have been at death's doors two times. I was born in a toilet chamber. At this time (1914) there were no bathrooms as such, and midwives were the attendants at births. My dear friend Alice Oliver told me that her mother had been the midwife when I was born. She had to dunk me in cold and then hot water to revive me and after a long time, I made everyone happy by giving out a healthy, strong cry. When we got ready to come to America, I was vaccinated and nearly died at sea from the vaccine. God has blessed me with good health ever since.

My parents made sure that we went to school faithfully. They were proud that their three children had graduated from high school. The teachers were patient with the Portuguese students and stayed after school to help them with their studies—remember, as children we could not speak English. My parents were very strict and I rebelled at times, but I do not regret this strict upbringing as it taught me to respect my parents and other people.

I married a United States Coast Guardsman of English, Irish and Indian ancestry on January 8, 1938. We have three children —Edward, James and Rosemary—and they all live on Cape Cod. We live in the home which my parents bought in 1925. It was in this house that I graduated from Provincetown High School in 1931 and got married from in 1938. My children were all born in this house; my mother, father and sister all died in this house —so it is part of my life with all its memories.

My husband Edward, my son Edward Jr. and my brother Manuel, 1943.

WHEN MY FATHER
FIRST CAME TO PROVINCETOWN...

When my father first came to Provincetown to go fishing, a fisherman's life was a very dangerous and strenuous one.

Early in the morning, around 4:00 a.m., he would walk down to one of the "stores sheds" which stood on the many piers that reached out into Provincetown Harbor in the late 1800s and early 1900s. Nets were mended and tall tales were told in these sheds; they also served as places for the men to warm up before going out to sea. The fishermen rowed out to their fishing boats in dories—the boats were not tied up at the pier as they are today; they would only do this to unload their catches or take on fuel.

George Elmer Browne

Sometimes if the weather was unsettled, the men would hang around on the piers, talking to other fishermen in their respective sheds until they either went home or out to sea. Many fishing trips were made when the catch brought home fetched a very low price; in these cases, the captain would often give the crew a little money out of his own pocket to buy food.

Most of the unmarried fishermen, and those who were married but had left their families in Portugal until they could afford to send for them, stayed in boarding houses called Casa da Comida e Cama, meaning "home with food and bed." These houses had rooms with two beds, some with four beds, per room and meals were included in the cost of $3.50 or $4.00 per week. There were local women who did the laundry for these men as a livelihood.

3

Several women married their customers—Uncle John says that is how he met his wife, our Aunt Cinny.

When Uncle John first came to America in 1905 from Gibraltar, he was ready to turn right around and go back because he wasn't making any money, and the "gold dollars" he had brought with him were quickly being spent. However, he soon started fishing on a schooner, a majestic many-masted sailing vessel that carried a crew of twenty men plus the engineer, cook and captain. The schooner would go out fishing for several weeks at a time. When the ship reached the fishing grounds, the men would get into dories in pairs and set out to fill their dories with fish to carry back to the mother ship

My father (left) and friend, 1907

until the ship's hold was full. In very rough weather the dories sometimes lost sight of each other and several men were lost at sea. After making a few trips, he decided this form of fishing was not for him, and he bought a two-man dory in partnership with his brother, my father. They fished for two years together until my father sold his share and returned to Portugal to get married.

Uncle John fished a few more years in the dory, and then bought the fishing vessel "Mary Magdalene," a fishing boat with captain, cook, engineer and one crew member. He captained this boat until he retired, but even then he continued to work in the Cape Cod Cold Storage fish packing plant in Provincetown (which stood on the site of the present Coast Guard station in town.)

When my father fished on the larger boats they would sail to Boston to sell their catch. He would come home with large sacks of sugar, flour and cornmeal, tubs of butter, lard and peanut butter and maybe licorice or molasses drops as a treat. He'd open the door with a big smile on his face as he knew he was bringing us enough food to last until he had a chance to go to Boston again.

My father would clean and dry codfish for the winter, when fresh fish might not be readily available. In those days many Portuguese families raised pigs and chickens and planted large vegetable gardens so they could have food for the winter months—my mother would bury carrots, cabbage and potatoes so they would keep through the winter. In the fall, the pigs were slaughtered. Linguica, blood sausage, pork shoulders and other cuts of meat were salted and stored as there were no refrigerators or ice boxes in the early 1900s.

My father was a fisherman all his life. He started fishing when he was 12 years old so he didn't get a formal education, but he was a good machinist and cook on the fishing boats he worked on. He made belts and bags out of string with fancy designs; today this craft is called macrame. He was a tall, good-looking man —we thought he looked like Clark Gable. He was a kind person and we children all loved him and of course respected him. He was patient but stubborn—if he said "It was black," it was black and nothing would change his mind.

My father insisted we eat our meals in a quiet atmosphere. However, we children would sometimes start to argue and he'd stop eating, look us straight in the face and say, unsmilingly, "Cala a boca i come," meaning "Eat and shut up."

My mother and father were both generous people—seldom did our dinner table consist of just the family. We were constantly inviting people in to eat with us. It seemed my mother, like so many Portuguese women, was always helping someone in need. She would say "What you give in charity is your sacred trust. Never let your right hand know what your left hand is doing."

My father with my sons Jimmy, 1½, and Eddie, 5.

My mother at age 63 with my daughter Rosemary, aged 5.

5

FOND MEMORIES OF
MY PROVINCETOWN

I remember Provincetown when it was a quaint little town with its tree-lined streets and its hollyhocks and rose gardens, and yes, its vegetable gardens.

Commercial Street in those days wasn't too commercial—it was a three mile stretch of stately trees and beautiful homes that their owners were so proud of. Many of these trees were destroyed in the 1944 hurricane and few were replanted. Grozier's Park (now the Boatslip Motor Inn) was a favorite spot for swimming or just relaxing by the green lawns and flower borders. We were able to just sit and watch the harbor and the boats. The reason this park was a favorite spot was because in those days there was no road out to New Beach (Herring Cove Beach). Commercial Street ended at the Provincetown Inn and from there the area was wooded so no cars or people could get by. The new road was cut through in 1934 and pedestrians and motor vehicles then had access to the six mile stretch of beautiful beach. No longer did vehicles have to turn back at the Provincetown Inn to return to the middle of town (Commercial Street was two-way then). When the road was first cut through, we called it the "New Beach" but during the Kennedy administration, the National Seashore acquired this stretch of beach and it became Herring Cove Beach. As teenagers, we would walk up to the breakwater in the west end of town and, if the tide was low, we would walk as far as we could on the large blocks of stone until the water was too high for us to jump from one rock to the other—just as you can see people enjoying themselves in this way today.

I remember the dances that were held in the winter every year in the Town Hall. Portuguese dancing was held in Caucus Hall, and American dancing was held in the main hall upstairs. These parties were free of charge and entire families attended. The children had as much fun as the grown-ups. I remember one incident that stands out in my mind at one of these dances . . . one of our dear Portuguese ladies lost her half slip while dancing the *Baile de Roda* (circle dance). She calmly picked it up and continued dancing, much to the chagrin of the more prim ladies and the cheering of the young people. After the dancing, we young ones were served ice cream downstairs in the basement where the Police Station is now. How I wish my children and the children

6

of today could have enjoyed so much simple fun!

I remember when several of the Portuguese fishermen had whisky stills. My father was not a drinking man but we had a still because it was cheaper to make the whisky for the holiday season than buy it, especially since we had Open House at Christmas time (the Portuguese kept their holiday until January 6th, the Day of The Three Kings). One day, someone told the fishermen that the "revenuers" were going to inspect all homes looking for stills. My father, as did his friends, wrapped his still in a burlap bag and dumped it out to sea. It came to light that this rumor was a hoax, and it was a hard pill to swallow. Apparently, this incident did not deter my parents from having their Open House that Christmas.

I remember walking to school in the deep, deep snow with boots up to my hips. We all had to walk to school because automobiles were far and few between. What fun we had on snowy days, especially when snowball fights took place. Sometimes Bradford Hill and Medelley Hill (by St. Peter's church) were closed to cars, although there were very few at that time, so that everyone, young and old, could go sledding. Owners of "double runners"

The double runner

would be in their glory riding on their homemade sleds with three and four sets of sleds pulling one long "accommodation". These sleds would hold 10 or more people. The best fun was riding from the top of the Bradford Hill as far as Winthrop Street and almost to Town Hall . . . but oh, how we hated trudging back up the hill, dragging the big sled behind us.

I remember the Pilgrim Monument during the Christmas season—it was a lovely sight with its four sides adorned with strings of colored lights glowing in the night, gently swaying in the breeze. Homes, yards, shops and streets, Town Hall, and even the Bas Relief were all gaily decorated, and prizes were given for the most beautiful display.

I remember the 200th anniversary of Provincetown in 1927. I have talked to several people who do not remember this celebration, but looking through old Town Reports, I found that in the report for 1925 a committee was to be appointed for this event. I remember the harbor was filled with all types of ships— U.S. destroyers, submarines, battleships, Coast Guard cutters. At night, the harbor was a galaxy of lights stretching across the bay; it was a sight that has never been repeated and probably never will be, and I'll never forget it.

I remember the Beachcombers' and Artists' Ball held in Town Hall every summer. I would go down to the Town Hall grounds and join the spectators lined up outside the entrance, cheering, sometimes booing, the costumes. I remember the artists with their folding canvas chairs and their easels sitting on the streets or at the beaches painting the beauty around them—the simple homes with their flower gardens full of roses, hollyhocks and sunflowers surrounded by freshly-painted picket fences.

George Elmer Browne

"Passers-by would stop to admire the work, or just shrug in bewilderment if they did not quite understand the modern style of painting."

My memory also takes me back to the Chinese Laundry which was located at 199 Commercial Street, now an antique shop. There were two, possibly three, Chinese restaurants in town then. Lai's was where Arnold's now is, and Wong's was where Plain and Fancy Restaurant is now. The Mayflower Restaurant is in the same spot as it was then. What is now the Marine Aquarium was Paige Brothers Garage, and Seamen's Savings Bank was Cape Cod Garage. Mr. Paige and George Ramos (he was a blacksmith where the Pied Piper Bar is now) ran open-air buses up and down Commercial and Bradford Streets for sightseeing—much enjoyed by us young people who often rode free of charge. The bus would go

as far as the Provincetown Inn in the west end of town, turn around and go back to West Vine Street to get on to Bradford Street, then down Bradford Street to the east end as far as the Tides Motel at the foot of Mayflower Heights and back up Commercial Street again. The buses were a bit on the hard side to get into, and when it rained tarpaulin would be dropped in front of each window.

There were wooden sidewalks in the West End of town in those days, as far as the Provincetown Inn. On the hill across the street from the Inn stood the "Castle", a house made of stucco and cement built in the early part of the century, the home of Joshua Paine. This house was later purchased by Carl Murchison, founder of the Journal Press. The house burned down at the same time as the first Moors Restaurant burned to the ground, destroying most of Murchison's famous art collection. I always wanted to go into the old house as it looked so mysterious; the romantic looking building became something of a fantasy to us young people. I did have the opportunity to go there as a Camp Fire Leader to teach the Camp Fire Girls group how to marbelize paper. The view of the dunes and the Harbor from the Tower Room was one I will never forget. After the fire, the Murchisons built a modern house which still stands on the site at the top of the hill.

George Elmer Browne

". . . there were wooden sidewalks in the West End of town in those days . . ."

9

I can remember when trains were a part of Provincetown. The depot was on Bradford Street, across from where the Mobil Garage is now. The freight trains went down to the end of MacMillan Wharf to load up with packed fish for the New York markets. As the train approached Commercial Street by the New York Store, a safety arm was lowered by one of the trainmen and no one could pass until the arm was raised and the train man waved you on. Where the beach taxis now park on Standish Street, the railroad tracks stood; the street itself was very narrow.

George Elmer Browne

Railroad Wharf, now known as MacMillan Wharf

I remember the night the High School burned to the ground in March 1930. The flames were spurting into the clouds high in the sky and the scene from our bedroom window was one of terror.

Before the fire.

My mother told me to go down to the corner of the street to ask a passer-by where the fire was. I'll never forget the large chips of burning wood falling in front of me as I ran. The neighbours and my brother, sister and I put out our garden hoses to wet down the roofs as large burning chips were falling everywhere. The wind carried some of them to the old Methodist Church (now the Provincetown Heritage Museum) causing a fire there, as well as in other buildings. I graduated from Provincetown High School

in 1931 but my class did not have a high school as the new school was not ready until the fall of 1932. Our class has had a class reunion every five years since our first one in 1951. We celebrated our fiftieth year on September 12, 1981 and we hope to meet again in 1986.

My graduation picture: I am in the front 2nd from right; my sister Jocelyn is on my left.

I remember the Boston boats coming in daily in the summer season, bringing hundreds of people to Provincetown to enjoy a delicious "shore dinner" (clam chowder, steamed clams, boiled lobster, corn-on-the-cob, fish, dessert and beverage for $2.95). The visitors would then trot out to explore the few gift shops and just enjoy the town until it was time to go back to the city. The Town Crier would stop at each restaurant before the visitors reached them to announce the number of passengers on the boats so that the restaurants could be prepared for their arrival.

George Elmer Browne

The Boston boat "Dorothea Bradford" at Railroad Wharf.

I also remember the Hurdy Gurdy man with his monkey. He would come down on the Boston Boat about twice a summer and walk along Commercial Street carrying the monkey on his shoulder. He would stop every so often and play his music box while the monkey performed tricks. The monkey would pass the hat around for donations and give the money to his master, then take off his hat and bow to the audience. The little monkey wore a red jacket and a little brimmed cap. My children used to love to go down when they heard that the Hurdy Gurdy man was in town, though some children shied away because they were a little frightened of the monkey.

I remember the "tar baby man". He was short and heavy-set. He drove a horse-drawn cart and tarred the streets. When we youngsters saw him coming, we would hang on the back of the cart and take a piece of tar to chew on, taunting him with "tar-baby, tar-baby" until he got really angry and shooed us off.

I remember when there used to be weirs for catching fish out on the waterfront. The trap boats would go out to the weirs every morning from April to December and would bring their catches to the pier for sale. When they had an abundant catch, they sometimes would have to make several trips to the pier. It was a special day for everyone the first time tinker mackerel were caught in the traps for this delicious fish was given away free down on the pier. One of the original trap boats, the "Charlotte", has been restored and is now housed in the Provincetown Heritage Museum.

George Elmer Browne

Weirs at the West End of Provincetown Harbor.

The captain of the "Charlotte" was Joe Oliver who still lives in Provincetown. At the close of the trap fishing season, the weirs would be picked up and the nets stretched out on land for the winter. Nets would be mended and the tall sticks would be replaced with new ones as needed. It was a sad day when the weirs were taken down for good because tinker mackerel were no longer plentiful; however, some are caught on the fishing boats today, and many people enjoy fishing for them from the end of the town pier.

I can remember when a large ship sank off Provincetown during the war in June of 1942 and the Civil Defense unit performed their duties so efficiently that they were presented the first citation and pennant given to any such organization. Survivors were brought to the New Central House (now the Crown and Anchor Motor Inn). All Civil Defense workers, Red Cross canteen and other volunteers tended to their needs. The cause of the disaster and the name of the ship were never disclosed. In February 1936 seven C.C.C. men from Eastham were rescued from an ice floe in Cape Cod Bay by the U.S.C.G. Harriet Lane stationed in Provincetown.

The ice floes were 19 feet high and it took several hours for the rescue to be completed. Provincetown recognized the feat of its base cutter by giving the officers and crew members a testimonial dinner. No special commendation was given them by the U.S.C.G. headquarters as this work had been in their line of duty.

Cape Cod Camp boys rescued from ice floe out at sea.

But most of all I remember the friendliness amongst neighbors who were always ready to help one another in times of need. I would like to share with you a very good example of neighborly love that touched my life and left me with a precious memory. In 1949 I bought a very large house on Winthrop Street, now the Watership Inn, which I intended to turn into a guest house. There were not too many houses for sale in those days. I had to move out of a five apartment house with no indoor toilet facilities and I had three small children, aged nine months, four years and eight years. My husband was then in the service and stationed in Buffalo, New York. The new house needed painting and papering inside and I needed to get it ready for the summer rental season to help pay the taxes and bills. I had signed the transfer papers on May 3, 1949 and my dear friends and neighbors spent several days helping me so I was ready for business on Memorial Day. Cook's Guest House was ready to welcome the many nice people I was to serve for 14 years. I certainly could never have done it alone, even with the help of my father, mother and sister.

The Cook Guest House, 1949 to 1963,
at 7 Winthrop Street.

My memories remain with me as time passes and I thank God that we still have our beautiful harbor, bright blue skies and fresh sea air. I pray that Provincetown's many residents and visitors will be able to enjoy its beauty for many years to come. I thank God for all the good memories of my early childhood and the opportunity to write this book. May you enjoy every page and cook many of the recipes which have sustained me and my family for so many years.

Mary Alice Cook
(Maria Alice Luiz)

SOUPS & APPETIZERS
SOPAS e HORS D'OEUVRES

Most Portuguese cooks make a kettle of soup nearly every day, as did my mother when I was growing up. I, too, still make many soup dishes and freeze what we do not eat immediately for a later day. Soups were our main meal at noon as our supper at night was usually fish. Meat was a luxury. On Sundays we had a roast of meat or chicken. Our Saturday noon meal was usually frankfurter stew or meat stew. I guess we didn't have many leftovers when I was growing up as we did not own a refrigerator or freezer. We did have an icebox—the iceman brought us a chunk of ice once or twice a week. In order to avoid spoilage of food, we only cooked as much as was needed for each meal.

I always use dried beans and soak them overnight. Canned beans may be used with nearly the same results, I suppose. Many of the soups I make use beans as they were cheap and full of protein. I'm sure my mother knew nothing about protein, all she knew was that they were good tasting and filled our stomachs.

Most of my recipes call for one pound of linguica (Portuguese sausage), but you may use more or less if you so desire. If linguica is unavailable, Italian pepperoni may be substituted at a pinch.

We usually eat Portuguese bread with our soups (the recipe follows later in this book) but Italian or French bread will serve as well.

Don't forget to taste the food several times while you are cooking it and add more spice or seasoning as needed.

SOUPS
SOPAS

Kale Soup or Turnip-Top Soup
Sopa de Couves or Sopa de Nabos

**4 lbs. kale or turnip-tops,
  fresh or frozen
2 lbs. white pea beans
1 lb. linguica or chourico
1 or 2 onions, chopped
4 potatoes, 2 whole and 2 cut up in pieces
1 or 2 carrots, diced, to add color
2 lbs. pork loin or other fat meat,
  or a pig's foot, fresh or smoked,
½ cup rice (optional)**

Soak beans overnight. Rinse well before cooking.
Wash fresh kale or turnip-tops and cut into small pieces. Place beans, linguica, meat, fresh kale or turnip-tops and onions in a large pot, cover with water and bring to a boil. Cook slowly. When meat and beans are fork-tender, add the kale (if using frozen), potato and carrot. Cook until vegetables are done, about 30 minutes (fresh kale may take longer to cook), adding more water as needed.

If you wish, you may add ½ cup rice to the soup. Simmer until the rice is cooked, stirring often to prevent the rice from sticking to the bottom of the pot.

Serve hot with plenty of fresh Portuguese bread.

Note: Chourico sausage makes a spicier soup.

Fish Chowder
Sopa de Peixe

½ lb. salt pork, cut into chunks,
    or bacon fat for frying
1 cup diced potatoes
4 cups water, or more if needed
1 cup milk
2 tablespoons flour
1 large onion, cut up
¼ lb. butter
2 bay leaves
1 small haddock, cod or hake,
    cut into small pieces
Paprika

Fry out the onion in the salt pork or bacon fat until it is lightly colored. Remove salt pork. Add fish, potatoes, bay leaves and enough water to cover. Cook until done—about 45 minutes.

Mix flour in milk, stirring well to avoid lumps (or shake in a bottle until smooth). Add to fish carefully, stirring slowly. Simmer gently for 5 minutes.

Add butter, sprinkle with paprika, and let stand a few minutes before serving.

George Elmer Browne

17

Red Bean Soup
Sopa de Feijao Vermelho

1 lb. red beans (soaked overnight)
  or 1 large can of red beans
1 large sweet potato, cut up in small pieces
2 medium carrots, chopped
½ lb. linguica, cut into 1" pieces
1 pork hock, or 1 lb. pork loin
  (more meat may be added if desired)
Salt and pepper to taste
½ cup vinegar (optional)

Put beans, linguica, meat and onion in a pot. Cover with water and cook until meat is fork-tender. Add vegetables. Cook until all ingredients are done. When necessary, add more water. You may add vinegar if you like a tart taste.

Note: if you like a heartier soup, add ½ cup macaroni for the last 20 minutes of cooking time. I do not use vinegar—the Azorean Portuguese like their food more on the tart side.

We ate this as a main noon meal, served with Portuguese bread and a pudding for dessert.

Red Beans with Chestnuts and Rice
Feijao Vermelho com Castanhas e Arroz

1 lb. red beans, soaked overnight
1 cup shelled dried chestnuts, soaked overnight
¼ lb. butter
½ cup long-grained rice
Salt and pepper to taste

Drain beans and chestnuts, rinsing out well. Place beans and chestnuts in a pot, covering them with water. Cook until they are soft.
    Add rice, salt and pepper. Cook until rice is done. Add more water during cooking if it is needed.
    Add butter and stir lightly. Let sit for a few minutes. Stir once before serving.

Note: we ate this soup mostly on meatless Fridays. These chestnuts may be bought at Italian stores.

Cabbage with Red Beans
Feijao Vermelho com Repolho

1 lb. red beans, soaked overnight
    or 1 large can of red beans
1 onion, quartered
1 lb. linguica, cut in 1" pieces
1 large carrot, chopped
1 large white potato, chopped
1 large sweet potato, chopped
1 very small cabbage
1 lb. pork loin or a pork hock (smoked or fresh)
6 or 7 cups of water
Salt and pepper to taste

Peel all vegetables and cut them up into small pieces. Cook all ingredients, except the cabbage, in a large pot with the water until they are done. Add the cabbage and cook for about twenty more minutes.
    You may add ¼ cup of elbow macaroni if you like a heartier soup.

Chick Pea Soup
Sopa de Grao de Bico

This is everyone's favorite!

3 cans of chick peas (ceci or garbanzos)
**   or 1 lb. dried chick peas soaked overnight**
1 lb. linguica (more if you wish)
2 lbs. lamb fores or pork loin
2 potatoes, chopped
1 large sweet potato, chopped
2 purple-top turnips, chopped
½ lb. squash (optional)
½ cup of rice
**   or 1 cup of elbow macaroni or spaghetti**
Salt and pepper to taste
Fresh sprig of spearmint (I freeze it for the winter)

Cover meat, linguica and onion with water and bring to a boil. Add the soaked, dried chick peas if you are using them. Cook until meat is fork tender—about 2½ or 3 hours over medium heat. When the meat is cooked, add the peeled and chopped vegetables (and the canned chick peas, if you are not using the dried kind). Add more liquid as needed while ingredients are cooking—I drain off most of the liquid when the soup is done and cook the rice or pasta in it.
    Add the sprig of spearmint for the last few minutes of cooking.

    Although you may eat this as a soup, in our family we used to eat the rice or pasta first and then eat the meat and vegetables on a plate as a main course. Any pasta or rice that is left over may be added to the left over soup and refrigerated—this soup also freezes very well.

Note: we always used to use the dried chick peas but found that some didn't seem to get soft enough even after soaking overnight, so now I use the canned peas.

Pea Soup
Sopa d'Ervilhas

2 16-oz. cans of peas (do not drain)
1 lb. linguica, cut up in 1" pieces
¼ lb. salt pork, chopped
1 onion, sliced
4 eggs in shells
4 cans of water (cans that contained peas)
1 large potato, quartered
Salt and pepper to taste

Saute onion and pork in a pot until onion is lightly colored. Add linguica, peas, potato and water.

When potato is cooked (about 20 minutes), make four "nests" in the soup and carefully break the eggs one at a time into the "nests". Cover and let simmer for a minute or two or until eggs are cooked.

Serve at once, putting one egg in each serving.

Note: if you wish, use 1 lb. of pork loin instead of salt pork for your meat ration of the day. When using pork loin, cook loin and linguica before adding the vegetables.

Use fresh peas for this dish when they are available.

21

Vegetable Soup
Sopa de Legumes

1 meat bone*
1 large onion, chopped
2 ribs celery, chopped
2 cans tomatoes
½ cup rice or thin noodles
You may also use any chopped-up left-over vegetables
    or two cans of diced mixed vegetables

Put all ingredients into a pot, add 6 cups of water and bring to a boil. Lower heat and cook until the meat is done.
    Wash rice and stir into soup. Cook for about twenty minutes. Let sit for 10 minutes before serving.

*Note: I seldom buy a soup bone because I buy a chuck roast and remove the bone with some meat, saving it for vegetable soup in the future.

String Bean Soup
Sopa de Vagens

1 lb. fresh string beans
    or 2 cans of string beans
1 large onion
4 or 5 bacon strips fried out (use fat only)
1 lb. linguica, cut into 1" pieces
1 large potato, cut up into pieces
5 or 6 cups of water, including water
    from canned beans, if using them
1 bay leaf
Salt and pepper to taste

Fry out the onion in the bacon fat in a large pot until it is lightly colored. Add beans to the pot and cook briefly before adding linguica and potato. If you are using fresh beans, cook beans until tender before adding other ingredients.

Add bay leaf and seasoning to taste and simmer until potato is cooked.

Note: I sometimes add a 2 lb. piece of pork loin to this soup to make it into a main meal. When the meat is cooked, carve it and ladle soup over the meat slices in a soup plate. A carrot may also be added to this dish to give a little color.

Tomato Soup with Toast
Sopa de Tomate com Torradas

8 tomatoes, chopped, skins removed
½ lb. salt pork, cut up in chunks
1 or 2 onions, sliced
2 green peppers, cut up
4 eggs in shells
Salt and pepper to taste

Fry out salt pork and saute onion and pepper in the fat until onion is golden. Remove salt pork. Add salt and pepper. Stir in the tomatoes and cook for about 10 minutes.

Make several "nests" in the tomato mixture and gently drop the eggs one at a time into each nest. Spoon juice over the eggs and cover the pot for a few minutes until the eggs have cooked. Serve on toasted Portuguese bread.

This makes a very light evening meal—it was a favorite of my friend Alice Oliver.

Chicken Soup
Canja com Arroz

1 whole chicken, or the gizzards,
   necks, hearts and backs of a chicken
1 large carrot, diced
1 large potato, diced
1 onion, sliced
2 ribs celery, chopped
½ cup of rice or thin noodles
Salt and pepper to taste
Fresh sprig of spearmint

Put all ingredients except the spearmint in a pot. Cover with water. Cook until the chicken is fork tender. If you are using a whole chicken to make soup, remove the chicken when it has cooked and eat it as a main course. (You may put the remainder of the chicken back in the soup when you have finished the meal.)

Add the rice or noodles. You may also wish to add a cube of chicken bouillon to the soup at this point. When rice or noodles are cooked, add the spearmint and turn off the burner. Stir a few times and remove the spearmint if you wish before serving.

Many of the Azorean Portuguese add a pinch of saffron to their chicken soup.

APPETIZERS

Horse Beans
Favas

1 lb. dry fava beans, soaked overnight
 or two cans of fava beans
2 cloves of garlic, chopped
½ cup olive oil (optional)
½ cup vinegar
Crushed red pepper
Salt and black pepper

Favas are large beans from the lima bean family. If you are using the canned favas, put all ingredients into a pot and simmer for 30 minutes. If using the dry beans, cook until done in water to cover. Drain and add above ingredients. Simmer for 30 minutes.

The seasoning of this dish is up to individual taste—if you like really hot food, then add more spices and vinegar.

These fava beans are served mostly as a snack or a party dish—serve in small dishes with toothpicks.

George Elmer Browne

FISH
PEIXE

Eating fish was a way of life in our home when I was growing up. We had boiled, baked, fried, stewed and marinated fish for our meals. I liked all kinds of fish except eels.

The ugliest but cleanest fish we ate was catfish. Catfish eat only shellfish. They have a dark, thick skin and an ugly face. But when it's skinned, the flesh is white and succulent.

It's hard to believe that the fish I scorned when I was growing up would be so difficult to get today, unless we buy it at the store. As my father was a fisherman, he brought home fish every day, and lobsters, scallops and crabs as well, when they were in season. Many times, he would bring the fish home all cleaned, ready to be cooked for that night's meal.

George Elmer Browne

Coming home with a fine catch of mackerel.

In my early days, Provincetown residents, and strangers also, would go down to the piers awaiting the return of the boats from the fishing grounds so they could get some free fish. The captains and their crews were most generous, and no one was turned away.

27

The captains still give fish away but not as generously as in the past because of the higher prices they get for their catch these days. So not too many old timers go down to the pier and ask for fish now.

When I lived in Missouri, I often wished I could taste a nice piece of fresh fish from the Provincetown fishing boats—recalling at the same time how I sometimes wished we hadn't had to eat quite so much fish when I was growing up.

Today, a piece of fish can cost as much or even more than a cut of meat. However, one consolation is that people may still dig for clams for a small fee (there is no charge for senior citizens). The license is available at Town Hall along with a ring that determines the size of quahogs (hardshell clams) you may take. If the quahog is small enough to go through the ring, you must rebury the clam so it has a chance to reach maturity. Digging for clams can be a tiring job, but if you are with friends, the job becomes an outing of fun.

My mother and father believed food cooked in its natural state had more flavor and was more wholesome—I heartily agree. What tastes better than a piece of fish fresh from the ocean, cooked to order?

My mother always fried her fish in olive oil, but since the price of pure olive oil is so high, I find vegetable oil will do just as well.

Baked Fish
Peixe Assado

1 whole haddock or cod fish
½ lb. salt pork, or 4 slices of bacon, cut in pieces
4 potatoes, peeled and quartered
1 large onion, sliced
2 bay leaves
2 tablespoons flour
Milk for basting
Paprika
Salt and pepper

Clean the fish, removing the head if you wish. Place fish in a large baking pan. Rub the fish with olive oil and cut slits on the surface with a sharp knife. Place pieces of salt pork or bacon in the slits. Scatter onion over the fish, and place potatoes in the pan around it. Sprinkle with salt, pepper, paprika and bay leaves.

Sprinkle two tablespoons of flour over the fish and place in the oven. Bake at 350 degrees for about 1½ hours, or until done, basting with milk frequently so the fish will not dry out.

Baked Stuffed Fish
Peixe Recheado Assado

Make a slit in the fish about 6"long and fill with your favorite stuffing. Sew up the sides and follow the above recipe.

Note: this dish may also be prepared with tomatoes—place sliced fresh tomatoes (or one can of tomatoes) over the fish and baste with tomato juice instead of milk.

Any fish left over may be boned and used for making fish cakes.

29

Baked Filet of Flounder
File de Linguado Assado

4 large flounder filets
¼ lb. butter
¼ cup bread crumbs
1 cup milk
Paprika
Salt and pepper

Butter a baking pan with half of the butter. Place the fish filets in the pan and top with the remaining butter. Pour the milk over the fish. Mix the bread crumbs with the pepper and salt and sprinkle them over the filets. Sprinkle with paprika.

Bake for about ½ hour at 350 degrees.

Note: you may add sliced onion and a can of tomatoes if you wish, but you might find you will be detracting from the delicate flavor of the fresh fish.

Do not use flounder filets that are too small because they tend to dry out while baking.

George Elmer Browne

Boiled Fish with Rice
Peixe Cozido com Arroz

1 fish, boned and cut up (cod,
    haddock, hake or mackerel)
1 onion, sliced
2 large potatoes cut into ½" rounds
1 cup of rice
½ lb. butter
Olive oil
Vinegar or fresh lemon juice

Place fish, onion and potatoes in a pot and cover with water. Simmer for at least 30 minutes or until potatoes are cooked. Drain off most of the cooking liquid and boil the rice in it in another pot.

When the rice is cooked, add the butter and stir in. Let the rice stand for a few minutes before serving. Stir once again just before serving.

If you wish, you may add the rice directly to the fish, onion and potato mixture (after the potatoes are cooked) and cook them together.

Note: in our family, we liked to eat the rice separately before we ate the fish.

Traditionally, this dish is eaten by placing the fish in a large deep serving dish and setting it in the center of the table. Each person then puts vinegar (or lemon juice) and olive oil in his own plate and adds fish and liquid from the serving dish.

Broiled Fish
Peixe Grelhardo

Use filet of flounder, haddock, cod, halibut
or swordfish

Enough fish to serve as many as you wish
    (If more than four, double recipe ingredients)
½ lb. butter
Bread crumbs as needed to cover fish
Juice of 1 fresh lemon
Salt and pepper
Fresh parsley
Paprika

Place fish (preferably fileted) on a pan lined with aluminum foil.
Cut butter into pieces and place on top of fish. Season fish and
sprinkle with breadcrumbs. Broil until lightly colored.
    Sprinkle lemon juice over the fish and broil for a few more
minutes. Serve hot, garnished with fresh parsley and sprinkled with
paprika.

Senora Alice's Codfish with Chick Peas
Bacalhau com Grao de Bico — Receita da Senhora Alice

1 lb. dried chick peas (ceci or garbanzos)
    or one can chick peas
2 lbs. dried salted fish
½ cup olive oil
1 clove garlic, crushed, or 1 teaspoon garlic salt
½ teaspoon ground black pepper
Vinegar (optional)

Soak the fish overnight, changing the water a few times if the fish tastes very salty.

Boil the fish, taste it, and if it is still too salty, change the water again. When the fish is cooked, drain and rinse it in warm water. If necesary, bone the fish, and replace fish in pot. Add other ingredients and cook for a further 20 minutes if you are using canned peas; longer if the peas were dried.

You may add vinegar to the pot or to individual servings for a tart taste. Fresh or canned tomatoes and onion slices may also be cooked with the fish and peas.

Mrs. Alice Oliver came to Provincetown from Olhao, Portugal, in 1915 on the same ship as I did.

George Elmer Browne

". . . [The fishermen] would clean and dry codfish for the winter . . ."

Marinated Catfish
Gato em Vinho d'Alhos

Catfish is one of the ugliest looking fish in the ocean. However, it is also one of the cleanest fish as it eats only shellfish. When skinned and cleaned, the flesh is pure white.

Marinade:
2 cups vinegar
2 cups water
½ cup sugar
1 teaspoon saffron
1 teaspoon red pepper
1 teaspoon black pepper, ground
2 cloves garlic, or 2 teaspoons garlic powder
2 or 3 bay leaves
1 tablespoon salt

Seasoned corn meal and flour
Olive oil for frying
1 tablespoon flour

Mix ingredients for the marinade in a deep bowl (do not use aluminum) and set aside.

Cut the catfish into slices but do not bone. Place fish in the marinade and let stand for at least 24 hours—more if you like a stronger flavor.

When the fish is ready to be cooked, drain off the marinade and set it aside for making gravy.

Shake the pieces of fish in a mixture of corn meal and flour in a paper bag. Fry quickly in hot olive oil. Place the fried fish in a deep casserole and keep warm, covering well to preserve the aroma until ready to serve.

Pour the marinade into a saucepan and add a little flour. Stir well and boil for a few minutes. Pour over the fried fish and serve immediately.

Fish Cakes
Bolinhas de Peixe

1 small haddock, cod or hake
2 large potatoes, peeled
2 eggs, slightly beaten
1 large onion, diced
1 tablespoon flour
Fresh parsley, chopped
Salt and pepper to taste

Boil the fish and potatoes together in a saucepan. Bone and flake the fish when it is cooked and mash the potatoes.

Mix the flaked fish and mashed potatoes thoroughly and add the beaten eggs. Mix well.

Add the diced onion to the fish mixture. Add the chopped parsley and seasonings and mix well.

Form the mixture into balls, flatten them and dust with flour. Fry in hot olive oil or vegetable shortening. Brown lightly on both sides and drain on paper towels.

These fish cakes are traditionally served with baked beans, though the calorie conscious may prefer a green salad.

Fish cakes of a smaller size make a good party treat—serve them cold and spear with a tooth pick, serving tartar sauce as an accompaniment.

Monkey Fish Stew (Links)
Macaco Guisado

1 monkey fish, dressed and
    cut into 3" pieces
1 can tomatoes, crushed (plus a can of water)
1 medium-sized can tomato puree
2 potatoes, peeled and quartered
1 onion, chopped
1 bay leaf
1 clove garlic, crushed,
    or 1 teaspoon garlic salt
Salt and pepper to taste

Saute onion in oil in a heavy pan until translucent and add tomatoes, tomato puree and a can of water. Add spices and stir well. Simmer for about 20 minutes.

Add fish and potatoes to pan and cook until the potatoes are done—about 20 minutes.

Taste the fish, adding more spices as needed. Add more water if necessary.

Note: I drain off most of the liquid and cook rice or elbow macaroni in it to serve as an accompaniment.

Monkey fish may also be fried or marinated.

Fish Cheeks and Tongues
Caras e Linguas de Peixe

1 lb. fish cheeks and tongues
2 eggs, beaten in one cup water
Flour, seasoned with salt, pepper and paprika
Olive oil for frying

Place seasoned flour in a paper or plastic bag. Dip fish into egg mixture, then into bag of flour.

Fry in hot oil and drain on paper towels.

Note: I also use cheeks and tongues to make fish chowder.

[This method of cooking fish is also perfect for swordfish, cut into small pieces.]

George Elmer Browne

Part of the great fishing fleet that once sailed out of Provincetown Harbor.

Baked Stuffed Quahogs
Ameijoas Assarde com Recheio

12 or more large quahogs (save shells)
½ cup chopped onion
1 lb. mushrooms, sliced
½ cup melted butter
3 tablespoons butter for topping and frying
2 tablespoons flour
1 teaspoon salt
½ teaspoon black pepper
1 cup fresh bread crumbs

Wash clams well to remove any grit and steam them in just enough water to cover. Remove clams and grind the meats, reserving the shells.

Saute onion and mushrooms in butter until they are soft. Blend in the flour and seasonings, stirring well. Add the ground clams and stir, cooking until the flour thickens. Set aside.

Mix bread crumbs with ½ cup melted butter. Butter the clam shells and fill with clam mixture. Top with breadcrumbs, sprinkle with paprika and dot with butter.

Bake in oven at 400 degrees for 10 minutes or until lightly browned.

This is a very filling but tasty dish. It is usually served as an appetizer or at parties.

Rice with Quahogs
Arroz com Ameijoas

12 or more small quahogs (hard-shelled clams)
1 cup rice
¼ lb. butter
¼ lb. salt pork, cut up in small pieces
1 onion, sliced
Pepper to taste (add salt only if necessary)

Wash clams well to remove any grit. Place clams in a heavy pot and steam in just enough water to cover. Steam until shells open and set aside.

In another pan, fry out the pork, add onion and saute slowly until golden brown. Add clam liquid and clams in their shells. Add the rice and cook it slowly in the clam liquor, stirring often. You may need to add more water from time to time.

When the rice is cooked, add the butter and pepper and stir. Turn off the heat and let the rice stand for about 5 minutes before serving.

For a change, you may substitute cornmeal for the rice, though it will take a little longer to cook.

Steamed Clams
Clams Cozide a Vapor

**Allow 12 steamers (soft-shelled clams)
per person as an appetizer
and approximately 20 or 30 per
person as a main course**
½—1 lb. butter, melted
Ground black pepper

Rinse clams well to remove sand and grit. Put clams in a deep pot and add water to cover. Steam clams for about 15 minutes, shaking pan to make sure all the clams are cooked. The steamers are cooked when their shells begin to open (beware of over-cooking shellfish).

Place clams, in their shells, in a large serving bowl. Strain broth and serve it individually in cups. Melted butter is also served individually.

Place serving bowl of steamers in the center of the table. Provide each diner with a large dinner napkin and a plate. Each person helps himself to clams from the center serving dish. To eat steamers, grasp one by the "snout" and peel off the membrane. Dip clam into broth to wash off any sand, then into the melted butter, and then pop into mouth. Bite off the steamer at the "snout" as sand sometimes is trapped in this part of the clam. ENJOY! ENJOY! (Mother always made us eat a slice or two of bread so we wouldn't get a belly ache.)

Note: For a clambake, cook linguica sausage and corn-on-the-cob with the clams as they steam. The linguica adds a spicy flavor to the clams.

You may also add hot sauce or red pepper flakes, crumbled linguica and/or chopped onion and parsley to the steaming clams for a different flavor, or you might like to steam them in white wine with a few cloves of chopped garlic.

Serve with plenty of freshly-baked Portuguese bread to soak up the broth and melted butter.

Clam Fritters
Fritura de Marisco

2 cups ground sea clams
1 cup flour
½ teaspoon baking powder
½ teaspoon pepper
½ teaspoon chopped parsley
1 onion, ground with the clams
2 eggs, beaten
Olive oil or other shortening for frying

Mix flour, pepper, chopped parsley and baking powder together. Add ground clams and onion and mix well. Add beaten eggs and mix well again.

Drop teaspoonsful of the mixture into hot fat. Fry until fritters are lightly browned on one side. Turn them and brown the other side. Drain and serve.

Always taste the first fritter to see if they need more seasoning.

Note: these clam fritters make a good meal accompanied with homemade baked beans and a green salad. They may also be served as an appetizer at parties, either hot or cold.

Oyster Stew
Ostras Guisadas

1 pint shucked oysters
½ teaspoon pepper
2 cups oyster liquid (add water if necessary)
2 cups milk
1 small diced onion
¼ lb. butter
Salt to taste

Strain oyster liquid to remove any grit. Thoroughly wash shucked oysters. Combine oysters and liquid and set aside.

Saute onion in butter lightly, add oysters and simmer for a few minutes. Add liquid, salt and pepper. Cook slowly for about 10 minutes. Add milk and heat through—do not let milk boil.

Sprinkle paprika on each serving of oyster stew.

Note: I usually add a large diced, cooked potato to the stew before adding the milk.

Scallop Stew
Molusco Guisadas

1 pint bay scallops
    or sea scallops, cut up
1 onion, sliced thinly
¼ lb. butter
1 quart milk
1 large potato, cooked and diced
    (reserve cooking liquid)
Salt and pepper to taste
Paprika

Fry out onion slices lightly in butter, being careful not to brown them. Add scallops and stir slowly. Simmer for a few minutes and set aside.

Add cooked potatoes to the scallops, then slowly add the milk. Simmer gently for about 10 minutes. Season to taste. Spoon into individual soup plates and sprinkle with paprika.

Scallop Casserole
Molusco Caçarola

1 lb. bay scallops or
 1 lb. sea scallops, cut into bite-sized pieces
1 cup cracker meal or crumbs
¼ lb. butter
Milk to cover
Paprika
Salt and pepper to taste

Place scallops and crumbs in layers in a casserole dish. Pour enough milk over scallops to cover them. Add seasoning. Scatter a few thin slices of butter on top, sprinkle with more crumbs, and top with more pieces of butter. Sprinkle with paprika.

Bake in oven at 350 degrees for about 25 minutes, and let sit for 10 minutes before serving.

I sometimes add grated cheese to this dish about 10 minutes before it is cooked.

Rice with Shrimp
Arroz com Camaroes

2 dozen medium-sized shrimp in the shell
1 cup rice
½ lb. butter
Salt and pepper to taste

Wash shrimp and place in a pot. Cover shrimp with water and simmer gently for a few minutes until shrimp are just cooked. Add rice and seasoning to shrimp and cook for about 20 minutes, adding more water if necessary. Stir well to prevent rice from sticking.

When rice is cooked, drain off any excess water and stir in butter. Serve while piping hot.

If you prefer, shrimp may be shelled before adding rice. You may also substitute corn meal for rice—it's delicious both ways.

When I was young, we had a cousin who lived in Georgia and one in Florida. They used to send us a barrel of shrimp on ice each Christmas. As the shrimp came here on the train, it had to be iced at various stages on its journey and at each stop handfuls of shrimp seemed mysteriously to disappear. So by the time the shrimp arrived in Provincetown there was barely half a barrel left, and after my mother had given some away to friends and neighbors, we were lucky to get two meals for the family!

Jocelyn's Baked Stuffed Shrimp

Camaroes Estofados cozidos no forno
favoritos de Jocelyna

12 Extra large shrimps in shells
**Stuffing (use your favorite stuffing recipe and add a little
seafood and white wine if you like)**
1 lb. of butter (melted - ¾ lb. might do it)
Onion flakes
Chopped parsley
Paprika

"Butterfly" the shrimp by splitting them in half as far as the tail
and flattening them. Remove the black cord and rinse the shrimp.
Stuff each shrimp and sprinkle a little onion and parsley on each
one. Pour melted butter on each shrimp (save a little for later).
Place shrimp on a cookie sheet and bake at 400 degrees for about
25 minutes.

Remove from oven and transfer to serving platter. Brush with
melted butter and lightly sprinkle with paprika. Serve with lemon
wedges.

Unloading lumber at Higgins' Wharf (now known as Macara's Wharf)

George Elmer Browne

Boiled Lobster
Lagosta Frevida

1¼ lb. lobster per person
Plenty of melted butter
Lemon wedges

Place enough water in a large pot to half cover the lobsters. When water has boiled, place lobsters in the water head first (putting lobsters in the refrigerator before cooking will chill them and they will feel nothing). Cover and boil until lobsters turn bright red and one of the small feelers breaks off easily (about 10 or 15 minutes depending on size; do not overcook or the lobsters will be tough). Remove lobsters to a platter and let water drain off before serving.

To eat a lobster: break off the large claws and crack them with a nut cracker. Pull or push out meat with a small lobster fork. Break head off from tail by grasping head in one hand and tail in the other and bending backwards. Break flippers off the end of the tail and push tail meat out of body with a pick or small fork. In the head you will find the roe and tamale—some people think this is the best part of the lobster, try it before you throw it out. If you are patient, you will find plenty of lobster meat in the head.

Dip each morsel in warm melted butter and sprinkle with fresh lemon juice. Delicious!

Lobster Salad:
Salada de Lagosta

I like to make lobster rolls and sandwiches. Add chopped onion, celery and mayonnaise to shredded lobster meat, just enough to hold the meat together (the meat found in the head of the lobster is ideal for lobster salad). Season with salt and pepper to taste and fill sandwich or roll.

Lobster Stew
Guisado de Lagosta

1 cup cooked lobster meat
½ cup butter
1 onion, diced
1 large cooked potato, diced
    (reserve cooking liquid)
4 cups milk
Salt, pepper and paprika

Saute onion in butter until soft and lightly colored. Add lobster pieces and stir to mix. Add potato and milk and stir. Add salt and pepper and heat slowly, being careful not to boil the mixture.
    Ladle into wide soup dishes and place a piece of butter in each bowl. Sprinkle with paprika and serve with pilot crackers.

George Elmer Browne

At the West End of Provincetown, opposite the Oldest House

MEAT
COMIDAS de CARNE

We had meat mostly on Sundays and holidays. On Christmas Day, we usually had a roast chicken or roast meat. Turkeys were extra special for Thanksgiving; for Easter Sunday we had roast chicken, or sometimes ham.

We would have roast pork and leg of lamb once in a while. There were several people who used to raise pigs and after they were fattened, they were butchered. I remember my mother buying pork shoulders and homemade linguica whenever she had the opportunity.

When I was growing up, the only meat we had was the meat used in the making of the many soups we ate, which were our staple diet. My mother used pork and lamb in most of the soups. I still use pork in my chick pea soup and kale soup.

We didn't know what it was to have hot dogs in buns, or hamburgers as they are known today. On Saturday night we sometimes would have frankfurters in a soup, or fried, with New England baked beans. I have included a recipe for this frankfurter stew in the following section.

Fishing boats tied up at Railroad Wharf, c. 1918

George Elmer Browne

Fresh Shoulder or Loin of Pork, Marinated
Lombo Fresco de Poco em Vinho d'Alhos

1 4-lb. loin or shoulder of pork
Marinade:
1 cup vinegar
1 cup red or white wine
2 cups water
2 large onions, sliced
1 small clove garlic, crushed, or 1 teaspoon garlic salt
2 bay leaves
Fresh chopped parsley
Red pepper to taste

Mix the ingredients for the marinade in a large enamel or china bowl and place the meat in it. Cover and let the meat stand for 24 hours or more. Turn the meat at least three times during this time.

Drain liquid from the meat and save it for basting. Place the meat in a roasting pan and roast it for 2½ to 3 hours at 350 degrees, or until the meat is cooked. Baste frequently with the marinade. The smell while the pork is cooking is delicious!

Note: if you would like potatoes with the meat, place them in the pot with the meat about an hour before the meat is cooked.

Linguica cooked over hot coals
Linguica Assada na Brasa

Use as much linguica as you wish cut into hot-dog bun lengths (we always ate the linguica on a hunk of Portuguese bread while I was growing up as we didn't have hot-dog buns.)
Put the linguica pieces on a long fork and cook over an open fire. Serve in hot-dog buns.

I thought I would share this recipe with you because of the increasing popularity of open fireplaces and wood-burning stoves.
Linguica rolls are popular enough to be sold at many food stands here in Provincetown in the summer. I think you would be able to buy linguica at most food stores on the East Coast.

Linguica Omelette
Omelet de Linguica

1 lb. linguica
8 eggs
½ cup milk
Salt and pepper
Bacon fat or shortening

Peel skin from linguica and crumble the sausage into small pieces. Put a little shortening into a frying pan, add the linguica and fry slowly, stirring.
Beat eggs, milk and seasoning together. When linguica is lightly cooked, pour the milk and egg mixture into the frying pan and cook as you would any omelette. I also like to add the beaten eggs and scramble them instead—but do not let the eggs cook too dry.

Serves 4.

Rosemary's Linguica Quiche
Quiche de Linguica a Moda de Rosemary

Basic recipe:
4 eggs and 2 cups light cream, beaten together
½ cup shredded Swiss cheese
½ cup shredded mild Cheddar cheese
¼ lb. linguica, skinned
dry onion flakes
8 slices bacon, fried crisp and crumbled
6 large or 12 small mushrooms, sliced
Pinch of salt and pepper
9" pastry pie shell, unbaked

Sprinkle the onion flakes into the pie shell. Add the crumbled bacon and linguica, the sliced mushrooms and the shredded cheeses. Season the egg and cream mixture and pour into the pastry shell.

Bake for 15 minutes at 425 degrees. Then lower the heat to 300 degrees and bake for a further 30 minutes or until the custard has set.

If you wish, you may use chopped cooked lobster meat, shrimp or other seafood instead of the linguica.

Ophelia's Portuguese Chicken Casserole
Caçarola de Galinha a Moda d'Ophelia

1 frying chicken, skinned and cut-up
1 medium onion, chopped
Several black olives
½ lb. linguica, cut in rounds
1 cup of rice
Olive oil for frying

Saute chicken pieces in oil with the chopped onion. Remove the chicken pieces when they are cooked and place them in a quart casserole and keep warm. Cook the rice in the remaining liquid, adding more water as necessary.

Spoon the cooked rice over the chicken pieces in the casserole, and arrange olives and linguica pieces around the chicken. Bake in the oven at 350 degrees until rice is lightly browned, about 15 or 20 minutes.

Smothered Chicken
Galinha Abafada

1 frying chicken, about 3 lbs., cut up in pieces
1 onion, sliced
1 clove garlic, crushed
½ lb. butter
½ cup vinegar or white wine
2 bay leaves
Saffron (optional)
4 small potatoes (parboiled and set aside)
Salt and pepper to taste

Saute onion and spices in the butter in a deep pot. Add the vinegar or wine and the chicken pieces. Cover with water and cook slowly for about 30 minutes. Add the parboiled potatoes and continue cooking until they are done.

Place the pot in the oven and cook just enough to brown the chicken lightly. Baste chicken frequently with the broth to prevent chicken from drying out.

Serve with rice.

Frankfurter Stew
Salsichas Guisadas

1 lb. frankfurters, cut into small pieces
1 large onion, sliced
1 tablespoons bacon fat or shortening
2 cans tomato paste or tomato soup
2 cups water
1 small clove garlic, crushed,
    or ½ teaspoon garlic salt
2 bay leaves
1 large potato, cut in eighths
1 whole potato
Salt and pepper to taste

Fry onion lightly in fat, add the frankfurters and brown. Add the tomato paste or tomato soup and potatoes. Cook slowly until done, stirring frequently to prevent sticking. Add more water as needed. Take the whole potato out of the stew, mash it and return to the stew to thicken it.

If you wish, you may drain off some of the liquid into a small pan and add ½ cup of rice or 1 cup of elbow macaroni. Cook, adding more liquid as necessary. We usually ate the rice or macaroni first, but you may add it directly to the stew if you wish.

This was often served as a noon meal, or a light supper on a Saturday night.

Meat Stew
Carne Guisada

1 lb. stewing beef or lamb
½ cup flour
1 onion, chopped
4 small potatoes, peeled and chopped
4 carrots, chopped
4 small purple-top turnips or
    1 very small white turnip
2 stalks celery, chopped
1 can tomatoes, optional
Salt and pepper to taste
Oil, vegetable shortening or bacon fat
    for frying onion

Dredge meat in flour. Fry out onion and meat together lightly over a low flame. Stir well while frying.

Add six cups of water to pan. Cover and cook for about an hour. Add vegetables and continue cooking until meat and vegetables are cooked. If you use the tomatoes, add them to the pot after browning the meat.

Serve with plenty of hot freshly-baked Portuguese bread.

Meat Loaf
Carne Mouida em Forma de Pao

1 lb. hamburger meat
1 onion, diced
1 egg
½ cup cracker meal or bread crumbs
1 cup milk or tomato juice
1 bay leaf
Salt and pepper to taste
Fresh parsley

Soak crumbs in either milk or tomato juice and set aside. Mix other ingredients thoroughly and fold in soaked crumbs. Spoon into a loaf pan and shape away from the sides of the pan.

Place pan in the oven at 350 degrees and bake for about 45 minutes. When cooked, remove meat loaf from pan and place on a platter.

Gravy: Remove excess fat from loaf pan and mix in one tablespoon of flour in pan drippings, stirring well to prevent lumps. Add one cup of water to pan and heat slowly, stirring constantly. If gravy is too thick, add a little more water as needed. Add salt and pepper to taste and a touch of Gravy Master for a little color if necessary.

For Country Gravy: Use milk instead of water and omit Gravy Master.

Note: for a complete meal, parboil potatoes and place them around the meat loaf before placing it in the oven.

Beef Liver
Figado de Vaca

1 lb. beef liver, sliced
½ cup flour
1 large onion, sliced
Oil or shortening for frying
Milk for dipping
Salt and pepper to taste

Dip the liver slices into the milk, then into the flour (I use a paper bag). Shake the liver free of excess flour.

Heat fat in a pan and fry liver and onions slowly, browning lightly on both sides. Simmer for about 10 minutes and season with salt and pepper.

Add 1 cup of water to make a light gravy and simmer for a further 5 minutes before serving.

Note: this was not the most favored of meals while I was growing up, but we had it at least twice a month. Even though we made funny faces, we still had to eat it—it was good for us, our mother said. It is not the most favored of our present meals, but I still cook it at least once a month.

George Elmer Browne

"Grozier's Park (now the Boatslip Motor Inn) was a favorite spot for swimming or just relaxing by the green lawns and flower borders. We were able to just sit and watch the harbor and the boats. The reason this park was a favorite spot was because in those days there was no road out to New Beach (Herring Cove Beach)." Page 6

Photographed at Grozier's Park is George Elmer Browne's brother Ralph, c. 1918.

BREADS & DESSERTS
PAES E SOBREMESAS

We didn't have many fancy desserts as I recall when I was a child, except at Christmas and on other special occasions. Our daily desserts were bread, tapioca or rice pudding. If eggs were cheap, we might have custard pie or baked custard.

My mother was a good cook but my father was the pie maker. He made us many homemade pies during the apple and berry season. Peddlers would come to the door selling apples and my mother would buy a bushel or more and store them in the circular cellar below our dining room. Potatoes, cabbage and onions were stored there, too. At Thanksgiving, we usually had squash or pumpkin pie, and once in a while cranberry pie, though we were not too fond of it.

Christmas time was my mother's turn to make delicious Portuguese sweets and Oh! how happy she was, despite the time and work she spent making them. She was in her glory during the Christmas season. I still remember the loving care she devoted to making these sweets — I think that must have been the secret ingredient that made them especially tasty because I don't think my Portuguese sweets taste as good as hers did!

"I remember the Pilgrim Monument during the Christmas Season - it was a lovely sight with its four sides adorned with strings of colored lights glowing in the night, gently swaying in the breeze."

These sweets took several days to make. My mother and her dear friend, Alice Oliver, would get together and help one another to make them. My sister Jocelyn and I would help to roll out the dough, a very tedious job as the dough had to be rolled out very thin and even on the pastry board. However, the hard work and time spent preparing these sweets was forgotten when my mother's face beamed with joy as she took them out of the oven ready to be enjoyed by all.

Left to right: My mother and her three dearest friends, Anna Coelho, Alice Oliver and Esther Guerriero, 1928.

On Christmas Eve, we held "open house" and we often had as many as 75 or 100 people visit us during the Christmas season. Troubadours came round to all the houses accompanied by musicians and sang songs to the "Meninho Jesus" (Child Jesus) at the beautiful altar my brother Mannie made every year. They would then eat and drink a little, and go on to the next "open house". When the troubadours knocked on the door they would ask "Ou meninho miza?", meaning "Does the child wet?"—in other words, "Is there something to drink in the house?"

My brother Mannie's Christmas creche.

My mother set up a very large dining room table covered with all the gorgeous sweets and drinks—there was homemade whisky and homemade wine. I still make many of these sweets and set a table at Christmas time, though not as elaborate as the one my mother prepared, to welcome anyone who might stop in, but somehow, the spirit of Christmas does not seem to be the same as it was in the past. I will always remember and cherish those truly blessed and beautiful Christmasses of my youth.

I am happy to share these family recipes with you and hope you will enjoy them as we did, along with our many friends, neighbours and guests who visited us on Christmas Eve and during the Christmas season. No one who came to our house during this time left without eating a sweet and maybe "just a little wine or liquor drink".

George Elmer Browne

View of Provincetown's waterfront showing three spires—Town Hall (right), the Universalist Church (left) and the church next to Town Hall (center—the spire no longer exists today and the church is now a cinema), c. 1915.

BREADS
PAES

Mamie's Portuguese Bread
Pao Portugues de Maria

Makes 3 loaves

8 cups unbleached flour
1 scant tablespoon salt
2 packets dry yeast
1 tablespoon sugar
¾ cup warm water for dissolving yeast
1 level tablespoon vegetable shortening
Warm water to mix dough as needed

Sift flour and salt together. Put yeast, sugar and ¾ cup warm water in a small bowl and stir to dissolve the yeast. Set aside.

Add shortening to flour and mix well. Add yeast mixture to flour. Add warm water sparingly and slowly, kneading dough thoroughly until it becomes elastic. Cover the dough and let it rise in a greased bowl for about 1½ hours. The dough should double its size.

Form three oval loaves, set them in greased bread pans, and let them rise again. Bake loaves in oven at 400 degrees for about 50 minutes or until golden brown. Portuguese bread should be eaten when fresh as it has a tendency to dry out.

Note: Mamie was eight years old when her mother taught her how to make this bread.

Sweet Bread
Lucy's Massa Cevada

This is a traditional Easter Bread made in most Azorean homes.

3 cups sugar
1 cup milk
½ lb. butter, melted
3 lbs. flour (not self-raising)
1 scant teaspoon salt
3 yeast cakes dissolved with 1 tablespoon
**   sugar and 1 cup warm water**
12 eggs

Beat sugar and eggs together. Add flour, salt, butter and milk. Add yeast mixture. Mix well and knead until dough is pliable. Let rise until double in size. Make into loaves or rolls. Let rise again until doubled in size. Bake at 375 degrees for about 40 minutes or until lightly browned.

For traditional Portuguese Easter bread, remove a small amount of dough from the top of each loaf before the second rising of the bread. Wash 6 eggs and place one egg in its shell in the hollow left in the dough. Form the piece of dough into strips and place over eggs to keep them in place while bread bakes.

I find that eggs boiled for a few minutes and cooled before placing them on top of the loaves will cook thoroughly while the bread is baking.

This bread is delicious, eaten toasted and buttered as well as plain.

Yield: 6 loaves or about 4 dozen rolls, depending on size.

Flippers
(Fried Dough)

Use Portuguese bread dough, or flipper dough from Provincetown's Portuguese Bakery—or you may use any bread dough. One loaf of dough will make about a dozen flippers. Cut dough into pieces (the pieces can be as large as you wish), stretch the dough a little and set aside for 10 minutes. Fry dough in hot oil, turning once or twice until each flipper is lightly browned. Drain on paper towels, or put flippers in a brown paper bag and shake.
Flippers are eaten with butter and maple syrup or molasses.

My father would sometimes go down to the Portuguese Bakery real early in the morning when the boat didn't go out fishing. He'd rush home with fliper dough, make flippers, and then come into our bedrooms and rub a flipper against our lips saying "Come on down and eat these while they are still hot, then you can go back to bed." You see, this would be about 5 or 6 o'clock in the morning. We would go downstairs, sleepy-eyed, eat all we could and then climb back in to bed. We certainly didn't want to miss out on this treat.
Today, a flipper fry is often given by school classes and local organizations as a fund-raising project—and they are always very successful ventures.

DESSERTS
SOBREMESAS

Portuguese Bread Pudding
Pudim de Pao a Moda Portuguesa

6 slices bread, buttered
1 quart milk, scalded
1 scant cup sugar
¼ lb. butter or margarine
4 eggs, well beaten
1 teaspoon vanilla extract
1 teaspoon cinnamon
¼ cup raisins, rinsed well in hot water
1 apple, peeled and chopped in small pieces
Pinch of salt
Nutmeg for topping

Scald milk. Cut the buttered bread into cubes and add to milk. Let stand for about 20 minutes. When the milk is cool, add the sugar, butter, salt and cinnamon and stir.

Fold the beaten eggs into the bread and milk mixture. Add the vanilla extract, raisins and apple and pour mixture into a buttered casserole dish. Sprinkle with nutmeg.

Bake in an oven at 350 degrees for about an hour. This pudding is quite solid—if you would like a softer pudding, place the baking dish in a pan of hot water in the oven while the pudding is cooking.

For variations, you may omit the raisins and add more apple, or add a few spoons of orange marmalade for a different flavor.

Some people like to top their bread pudding with a layer of soft meringue.

Portuguese Sweet Rice Pudding
Pudim d'Arroz Douce

½ cup rice, rinsed well
½ cup sugar
3 egg yolks and 1 whole egg, beaten
    together lightly with a fork
1 cup milk, scalded
1 teaspoon lemon extract
2 cups boiling water
½ teaspoon salt
Cinnamon
1 piece of lemon peel

Add the rice and lemon peel to 2 cups of boiling water and stir well. Cover and simmer for 20 to 25 minutes, stirring constantly to prevent sticking and burning—the rice will be nearly dry when cooked. Set aside while you scald the milk.

Return rice to the fire, add the sugar and mix well. Then gradually add the scalded milk and stir. Simmer for about 10 or 15 minutes, stirring constantly, until most of the milk has been absorbed. Add the beaten eggs, folding them in thoroughly.

Remove the rice from the fire and add the lemon extract. The pudding will be on the dry side. Spoon the pudding into individual dessert dishes and sprinkle with cinnamon. Rice pudding is good served warm or cold topped with whipped cream.

This pudding needs patience to cook correctly as constant stirring is necessary to prevent the rice from sticking to the pan.

Portuguese Caramelized Custard
"Flan"*

1 cup sugar (for caramel)
6 eggs
½ cup sugar
2 cups milk, heated
1 can condensed milk mixed with 1 cup warm water
    or use two cups light cream
2 teaspoons vanilla extract or other flavoring
½ teaspoon salt

Put one cup of sugar in a heavy skillet and cook over medium heat until the sugar melts. Stir until the sugar is light brown and caramelizes. Pour caramel into individual custard cups and swirl the liquid so the sides and bottom of the cups are covered. Set cups aside

Beat the eggs slightly and add ½ cup sugar, the salt and flavoring. Add the heated milk slowly, stirring well.

Pour the mixture into the custard cups over the caramel and place the cups in a baking pan. Pour an inch of water into the pan and place in oven. Bake at 350 degrees for about 35 to 40 minutes or until custard is set (when a knife tip inserted in custard comes out clean).

Allow custard to cool before serving, but do not put the pudding in the refrigerator. If you wish, you may turn this pudding out onto dessert plates.

Note: My mother did not make this pudding very often, probably because eggs were not very plentiful unless you raised your own chickens.

*In restaurants today, a pudding similar to my mother's, called *flan*, is often served. Brandy, wine or other flavoring is added to the custard before baking. I do not think *flan* is a true Portuguese name for this pudding as I cannot find the word in my dictionary, and none of my Portuguese friends are familiar with it either. Flan is a dessert which is found in Spanish, French and Italian cooking.

DESSERTS FOR CHRISTMAS AND SPECIAL OCCASIONS
Sobremesas de Natal e Outras Ocasioes Especiaes

The following recipes were made for Christmas, Baptisms, Weddings and other special occasions.

Rolled Cookies
Boles de Folha

(my favorite—these are very rich, but if you are like me, you will eat several as you bake them. Have fun!)

5 lbs. flour (not self-rising)
1½ cups sugar
2 teaspoons salt
7 eggs, beaten
1 lb. butter
1 lb. lard
1 cup orange juice, or more if necessary, warmed
2 packets dry yeast dissolved in ½ cup warm water
and 1 tablespoon sugar

Filling:
1 lb. melted butter (use while warm)
5 lbs. sugar (you may need more, or you may use less)

Melt 1 lb. butter with 1 lb. lard. Put flour, 1½ cups of sugar and salt in a very large pan—I use a white enameled pan. Add the beaten eggs, butter and lard mixture and the yeast. Mix the dough with you hands and add the warmed orange juice. Knead the dough well until it is all well mixed in. Knead it as you would knead bread, until dough leaves the sides of the pan. If it looks as if the dough isn't forming, take heart and keep mixing it until you've won. When mixed, let the dough rest for at least 20 minutes.

Extra dough may be stored in the freezer for later use, or if you wish to make the cookies the next day, you may leave the dough in the refrigerator overnight. Let it get soft before using it.

Take a ball of dough, roll it out to the length and width of a pie board and cut off the ragged edges. With your hands, spread melted butter over the dough. Sprinkle sugar over the entire buttered area, spreading it with your hands and patting the sugar down.

Roll the dough up like a jelly roll, a little on the tight side. Cut the roll into one inch pieces and place them on an ungreased cookie sheet, close together. Tuck any loose ends under the roll.

Let the dough rise until it is soft to touch and the butter is starting to melt. Cover with towels to keep the dough warm.

Preheat oven to 325 degrees and bake cookies until they are lightly colored, about 25 minutes. Remove them from baking pan immediately, otherwise the melted sugar will stick to the pan. Turn the rolls upside down to help dry them out.

These are especially delicious when newly made; however, I have stored Boles d'Folha made at Christmas time in a plastic bag in a coffee can and they were still good in February. If by chance they may seem a little hard to bite into, you might like to dunk them in hot coffee or tea, or you can wrap them in foil and reheat in the oven.

Makes approximately 10 dozen.

Christmas creche at St. Peter's Church, 1930.

Sweet Potato Turnovers
Trutas

4 lbs. flour (not self-rising)
1 cup sugar
1 lb. butter
1 lb. lard (do not use vegetable shortening)
1½ cups warm orange juice, more if needed
2 jiggers whisky or red wine
    mixed in 1 cup warm water

Melt butter and lard together.

Put flour in a deep pan—I use a white enameled dish pan. Make a well in the flour with your hands and place all the other ingredients in this well. Work dough with hands until it feels soft and leaves the side of the pan.

Roll out the dough on a pastry board, a bit on the thin side. Cut out circles with a 3" pastry cutter and place a tablespoon of sweet potato mix (recipe follows) in the dough circles. Fold the dough over like a turnover. Use a pastry wheel to close each one, pressing down so truta won't open when it is being fried.

Fry trutas in deep fat, drain and let cool. When cool, shake turnovers lightly in a bag of powdered sugar.

You may prefer to use honey instead of sugar—warm some honey mixed with a little water and lemon juice and place in a pan. Dip the trutas in the mixture so they are coated, and eat them at once or they will become very sticky and hard to take off the serving dish.

Sweet Potato Filling

4 lbs. sweet potatoes, cooked and peeled
1½ teaspoons lemon extract
    or fresh lemon juice, or concentrated juice
1 teaspoon grated lemon peel
1½ teaspoons cinnamon
1 cup sugar

Mash sweet potatoes. Mix potatoes and all other ingredients in a pan. Stir over a low fire until the sugar has dissolved. Taste to see if more sugar is needed. The mixture should be a dark color when it is cooked—be sure to stir constantly so potato won't stick or burn.

Note: Left-over dough and filling can be frozen to be used at a later date. Sometimes I like to bake the trutas instead of frying them.

My mother used to say that the truta was drunk (estar bebida) because the dough took the alcoholic beverage. The red wine tends to make the truta dough a little darker than the whisky does.

These trutas are as much of a favorite with the non-Portuguese of Provincetown as they are with the Portuguese—trutas, along with many other Portuguese pastries, may be purchased at Provincetown's Portuguese Bakery on Commercial Street.

Makes approximately 10 doz.

Almond Cookies
Bolos d'Amendoas

3 egg whites
1 heaping cup sugar
2 cups bread crumbs (day-old bread)
2 cups ground almonds
2 tablespoons melted butter
2 teaspoons almond extract
Blanched almonds for decoration

Put all ingredients except egg whites into a deep bowl and mix well. Beat egg whites until they reach a peak and fold them into the almond mixture. Blend all ingredients well.

Drop teaspoonsfull of the mixture about an inch apart onto a lightly greased baking sheet. Top each bolo with a sliver of blanched almond. Bake at 325 degrees until golden brown.

Makes approximately 3 dozen.

Egg Cookies
Spreciones (Rosemary's Favorite)

1 cup sugar
2 cups flour
6 egg yolks (use egg whites to make Suspiros)
2 whole eggs
¼ teaspoon salt
Peel of one lemon, grated
1 beaten egg & almond slivers for topping

Beat sugar, eggs, salt and lemon peel until mixture thickens. Add flour gradually until mixture is thick but not dry.

Roll into small balls in the palm of your hand and form a small peak in each ball with your fingers. Place the cookies on a baking sheet with the peaks pointing upwards. Brush with beaten egg and top with an almond sliver.

Bake at 325 degrees for about 20 minutes. Cool before removing from baking sheet.

Note: these cookies should be eaten while fresh as they tend to get hard quickly—though they do taste good when hard, especially dunked in coffee.

Dreams
Sonhos

1 cup flour (not self-rising)
¼ teaspoon salt
1 tablespoon butter
1 cup water
6 to 8 eggs at room temperature

Boil water, butter and salt together. Add flour slowly, stirring constantly until ingredients are well blended and mixture forms a soft dough.

Drop teaspoonsful of the mixture in hot oil. Pierce with a fork and turn the balls until they are lightly browned and partially opened. Drain on paper towels or shake in a brown paper bag.

When ready to serve, dip cookies in melted, hot honey or shake in powdered sugar.

Note: These will not keep well, so enjoy them while they are fresh. The dough these are made with is like cream puff dough— unfortunately, I don't have much luck making these delicious cookies.

Sighs
Suspiros

1 heaping cup sugar
3 egg whites (at room temperature)
Pinch of salt
Lemon or almond flavoring

Rinse a large bowl in hot water. Place all ingredients in bowl and beat with a mixer at high speed until mixture stands in stiff peaks.

Line a cookie sheet with a paper bag cut to fit without wrinkles. Drop small teaspoonsful of the mixture onto the cookie sheet, swirling them as they drop to form a prettily-shaped top.

Bake at 325 degrees until lightly colored. Take out of the oven carefully and cool for at least 5 minutes. Remove from cookie sheet.

These cookies are especially delicious when ground nuts, grated coconut or chocolate bits are added to the mixture after it is beaten.

Note: I had to beat this mixture by hand when I was young as we had no electric mixer. My mother would stand by to make sure I didn't stop beating because she did not want the mixture to lose the "ponte", or the stage where she knew it was beaten enough. If the mixture will not stand up, it has not been beaten enough.

Makes approximately 4 dozen.

George Elmer Browne

CAPE COD FAVORITES

Having lived in Provincetown over a half century and then some, I'd like to share a few of the recipes that are a great part of our lives here on Cape Cod.

The best part of making some of these recipes is that you can go out and gather your own ingredients—cranberries, beach plums, blueberries, clams.

I hope you enjoy these recipes as much as the Portuguese recipes.

George Elmer Browne

New England Baked Beans
Feijao Assado

3 cups white pea beans
2 teaspoons salt
½ cup molasses
2 tablespoons brown sugar
1 teaspoon dry mustard
½ lb. salt pork
1 whole onion
Boiling water to cover

Soak beans overnight. Drain water from beans, add fresh water and bring to a boil. Cook until beans shed their skins. Drain. Place salt pork, cut into three pieces, in the bottom of a bean pot. Top with the onion. Add the beans and seasonings. Cover with boiling water.

Bake beans in a slow oven (250 degrees) for about 6 to 8 hours or until they are cooked. Stir occasionally. Do not let the beans dry out; add more water if necessary—however, do not let the beans get too soupy, either.

Let stand at least 30 minutes before serving. Serve with fried linguica and potato salad, or as a vegetable with any meat dish.

When I was growing up we used to cook baked beans in the wood/coal stove, slowly all night, and usually ate them on a Saturday with linguica or frankfurters.

Pot Roast Boneless or bone-in chuck
Carne Assada

4 lbs. beef (inexpensive cut)
1 tablespoon oil
2 onions, sliced
4 small carrots
4 small potatoes
4 small purple-top turnips
½ teaspoon garlic salt
1 bay leaf
Salt and pepper

Place meat in a pot with the oil and brown it on all sides. Add salt and pepper, onions and garlic salt. Add water to barely cover the meat and add the bay leaf. Cover and cook slowly until meat is fork tender (about 3 hours). Add vegetables and cook until they are done.

If necessary, add more water—not too much, just enough to make a gravy.

Apple-Raisin-Cranberry Pie

1 cup apples, thinly sliced
1 cup cranberries, chopped
½ cup raisins
1 cup sugar
1 tablespoon flour or tapioca
1 cup hot water
1 teaspoon vanilla or almond flavoring
9" pie crust, uncooked, and extra dough for topping

Mix all ingredients, except flavoring, and cook for about 15 minutes in a saucepan. Remove from heat, add flavoring and stir in. Leave to cool for about 10 minutes. Pour cooled mixture into a 9" pie crust, top with pastry lattice and bake in oven at 350 degrees for 30 minutes. Or you may prefer to bake the pie without a pastry topping and place a layer of meringue on top of the fruit and brown lightly.

George Elmer Browne

Blueberry Pie

1 quart blueberries
½ cup sugar
1 tablespoon flour or tapioca
½ teaspoon cinnamon
½ teaspoon lemon juice
¼ lb. butter
Pinch of salt
9" pie crust with pie-crust cover

Rinse blueberries in cold water. Mix together the flour, sugar, cinnamon and lemon juice. Place the berries in a pie crust, sprinkle on the flour/sugar mixture, cut the butter into small pieces and place on top of the berries.

Place pie crust on top of the berries and crimp around the edges of the pie, sealing well so juice won't seep out. Brush the top with milk and make a few cuts in the pastry top. Bake for about 35 minutes in the oven at 350 degrees. Serve topped with vanilla ice cream.

Beach Plum Jelly

2 quarts beach plums (to yield approx. 4 cups juice)
4 cups sugar

Cook beach plums in a pot with 2½ cups of water and strain through a clean cloth to obtain clear juice. Mix the juice and sugar well and bring to a boil. Cook, stirring constantly, until the syrup stage is reached (when a drop of hot liquid dropped into a saucer of cold water has a jelly-like consistency). Cook for a few more minutes, remove from the heat and skim off any foam. Pour the jelly into scalded jelly glasses or jars. Cover with melted paraffin wax.

This is the old-fashioned way of cooking beach plum jelly. I find it tends to become too solid if overcooked, so I prefer to use pectin.

Note: NEVER heat paraffin over a direct flame—always put paraffin in a double-boiler or in a saucepan over a pan of hot water.

Beach Plum Jelly using Pectin

Certo packages no longer carry the recipe for beach plum jelly or jam so I thought I would share these recipes with you.

2 quarts beach plums
**   yielding 3½ to 4 cups juice**
6 cups sugar
½ bottle Certo

Place 2 quarts of beachplums in a pot with 2½ cups water. Cook for about 25 minutes, mashing the plums carefully, being careful not to get burnt by hot splashing juice. Strain mixture through a clean cloth. Do not squeeze the cloth otherwise the jelly will become cloudy. Just leave it to drip slowly.

Mix juice and sugar and bring to a boil. When a rolling boil is reached, add the Certo. Boil hard for two minutes, stirring well. Remove the jelly from the heat and skim off any foam.

Pour hot jelly into scalded glasses or jars and seal with paraffin wax.

Leave the jelly to set until it is cold. Wait a day or two before using.

Beach Plum Jam

6 cups beach plums
    to yield approx. 4 cups pulp
7 cups sugar
1 package Certo or Sure Jell

Clean berries and cook them. Place cooked berries in a sieve and mash them through to make pulp. Make sure the holes are small enough to prevent pits falling into the pulp. This is a very tedious job.

Put pulp and sugar in a large, heavy pot and cook until mixture boils. Cook for 5 minutes. Skim off foam (you may have to skim more than once), let cook for 2 minutes and pour jam into scalded glasses or jars. Cover with melted paraffin wax.

This is my favorite—I would rather eat beach plum jam than beach plum jelly.

RECIPES FROM MY FRIENDS

When rereading my recipes, I thought: Wouldn't it be nice to include favorite recipes of some of my friends. I have too many friends, I could not possibly use all their recipes, so I have asked a few of them to give me the folowing recipes, which are varied and I know you will enjoy them. A few of my friends' recipes also appear throughout this book. I thank them all for allowing me to publish their recipes.

I have a trivet that says:

> Count your life
> By smiles, not tears
> Count your age
> By friends, not years.

Am I a lucky person? I think so.

Helen, Mary, Nellie and myself.

Anna's Beach Terrace Chili

6 large onions, chopped
6 large cloves garlic, minced
1 cup corn oil
2 large green peppers, chopped
3 lbs. ground beef
3 large cans tomato puree
3 large cans of Friends red kidney beans with pork

In a large kettle, place oil, onions, garlic and green peppers. Saute until onions are soft. Add ground beef and brown. Add tomato puree and red beans.

Stir together well and add approximately one tablespoon of salt, or to taste. Lower flame on burner and stir in one teaspoon of chili powder. Cook, stirring over a low flame for one hour.

This chili tastes even better reheated the next day.

Irene's Porcupine Meat Loaf

1½ lbs. hamburger meat
½ cup uncooked rice
1 large onion, diced
1½ teaspoons salt
¼ teaspoon black pepper
1½ teaspoon poultry seasoning
1 teaspoon Worcestershire sauce
2 bouillon cubes dissolved in 2 cups hot water
¼ cup flour
½ cup water

Thoroughly mix meat, rice, onions, ½ cup of water, poultry seasoning, Worcestershire sauce, salt and pepper together. Shape into a round loaf and put into a 2 quart casserole. Pour dissolved bouillon cube liquid over loaf. Cover and bake in oven at 350 degrees for about 2 hours.
Remove loaf to a platter. Thicken liquid in casserole dish with the flour and ⅓ cup of cold water and serve with meat loaf.

Jocelyn's Peanut Butter Fudge

4 cups sugar
1⅓ cups milk
2 teaspoons vanilla extract
1 18-oz. jar peanut butter, crunchy if you like it
4 large tablespoons marshmallow fluff
Pinch of salt

Mix sugar, salt and milk together. Cook the mixture until it reaches the soft ball stage. Continue cooking for twelve minutes, or use a candy thermometer if you have one.
Add vanilla extract, peanut butter and marshmallow. Beat until thick but do not overbeat otherwise the fudge will get too thick and harden before you can spread it in the pan. Pour mixture into a square, buttered pan and cut into squares.

My sister Jocelyn used to make this for all the local food sales that she donated food to. Her favorite was the Rescue Squad summer sale for which she made several batches of this fudge—it sold like hot cakes.
I may be a good cook, but I cannot make fudge fit to eat.

Mary's Apricot Squares

1 cup sugar
2 cups plus 1 tablespoon flour
3 oz. margarine, melted
1¼ cups grated coconut
½ cup ground walnuts
¼ teapoon salt
1 egg
1 teaspoon vanilla extract
12 oz. apricot preserves

Mix dry ingredients well, including nuts and coconut. Make a well in the mixture and add the melted margarine, egg and vanilla extract. Mix with a fork until a dough forms.

Place half of the dough in a square 9 inch pan. Spread apricot preseves over dough mixture. Sprinkle remaining dough over the preserves. Bake at 350 degrees for 35 minutes. When cool cut into squares.

I am on the left, with my friends Edith, Cliff, Phil, Helen & Polly, 1933. We worked together at the "Blue Moon Cafe", which was located on Standish Street where the taxi stand is now. I waited on tables in the summers while I was in high school.

INDEX

SOUPS & APPETIZERS

Cabbage with Red Beans 19
Chick Pea Soup 20
Chicken Soup 24
Fish Chowder 17
Horse Beans (Favas) 25
Kale Soup 16
Pea Soup 21
Red Beans with Chestnuts and Rice 18
Red Bean Soup 18
String Bean Soup 22
Tomato Soup with Toast 23
Turnip Top Soup 16
Vegetable Soup 22

VEGETABLES

New England Baked Beans 76
Horse Beans (Favas) 25

FISH

Baked Fish 29
Baked Stuffed Fish 29
Boiled Fish with Rice 31
Broiled Fish 32
Catfish, Marinated 34
Clam Fritters 41
Clams, Steamed 40
Codfish with Chick Peas 33
Fish Cakes 35
Fish Cheeks & Tongues 37
Flounder, Baked Filet of 30
Links 36
Lobster, Boiled 46
Lobster Salad 47

Lobster Stew 47
Monkey Fish Stew...................................36
Oyster Stew 42
Quahogs, Baked Stuffed 38
Quahogs, with Rice.................................39
Scallop Casserole 43
Scallop Stew 42
Shrimp, Baked Stuffed 45
Shrimp, with Rice 44

MEAT

Beef Liver 57
Chicken Casserole...................................52
Chicken, Smothered 53
Chili...83
Frankfurter Stew....................................54
Linguica, cooked over hot coals 51
Linguica Omelette...................................51
Linguica Quiche 52
Meat Loaf 56
Meal Loaf, Porcupine 83
Meat Stew 55
Pork, Marinated Shoulder or Loin....................50
Pot Roast 77

BREADS

Flippers (Fried Dough) 64
Portuguese Bread 62
Sweet Bread 63

DESSERTS

Almond Cookies 71
Apple-Raisin-Cranberry Pie..........................78
Apricot Squares.....................................85

Blueberry Pie 79
Dreams (Sonhos) 72
Egg Cookies (Spreciones) 72
"Flan" 67
Peanut Butter Fudge 84
Portuguese Bread Pudding.........................65
Portuguese Caramelized Custard 67
Portuguese Sweet Rice Pudding.....................66
Rolled Cookies (Boles) 68
Sighs (Suspiros) 73
Sweet Potato Turnovers (Trutas) 70

PRESERVES

Beach Plum Jam 81
Beach Plum Jelly.................................80
Beach Plum Jelly made with Pectin..................80